LIVING IN GOD'S HOUSE: HIS DESIGN IN ACTION

BY BRIAN JOHNSTON

Copyright © 2016 HAYES PRESS

All rights reserved. No part of this book may be reproduced, stored in a retrieval system, or transmitted in any form, without the written permission of Hayes Press.

Published by:

HAYES PRESS CHRISTIAN PUBLISHERS

The Barn, Flaxlands

Royal Wootton Bassett

Swindon, SN4 8DY

United Kingdom

<u>www.hayespress.org</u>

Unless otherwise indicated, all Scripture quotations are from the New American Standard Bible® (NASB®), Copyright © 1960, 1962, 1963, 1968, 1971, 1972, 1973, 1975, 1977, 1995 by The Lockman Foundation. Used by permission. (www.Lockman.org)

Scriptures marked NKJV are from the HOLY BIBLE, the New King James Version® (NKJV®). Copyright © 1982 Thomas Nelson, Inc. Used by permission. All rights reserved. Scriptures marked NIV are from the New

International Version®, NIV® Copyright © 1973, 1978, 1984, 2011 by Biblica, Inc.™ Used by permission. All rights reserved worldwide.

Digital ISBN: 9781911433088

Print ISBN: 9781911433071

First Edition June 2016

10 9 8 7 6 5 4 3 2 1

If you enjoyed reading this book and/or others in the series, we would really appreciate it if you could just take a couple of minutes to leave a brief review where you downloaded this book.

CHAPTER ONE: PLANTED TOGETHER IN GOD'S GARDEN

As we begin our look at what it means to live in God's house, we're going to consider something which the Bible tells us that God really wants for all Christians. Using the analogy of a garden, God illustrates the fact that he doesn't want believers to be isolated from one another after they've been born again. Instead, he wants them to be gathered together in a similar way to how you or I might bring plants we've selected from various places and plant them together in the way we want in an organised garden setting.

This desire of the Lord Jesus for the togetherness of those who would come to believe on him was most clearly expressed in the prayer for Christian unity which he voiced in John chapter 17, shortly before he went to the cross to die. He prayed:

"I do not ask on behalf of these alone [referring to his Apostles], but for those also who believe in Me through their word; that they may all be one; even as You, Father, are in Me and I in You, that they also may be in Us, so that the world may believe that You sent Me. The glory which You have given Me I have given to them, that they may be one, just as We are one..." (John 17:20-22)

The greatest desire of our Lord Jesus is obvious: it's for Christian unity. It's quite sublime to think that, by the Spirit's operation, it's possible for Christians to co-operate together in a similar way to the Lord and his Father. John's Gospel emphasizes how our Lord was remaining in the Father and the Father was also remaining in him, as the Lord performed his Father's works (John 10:38; 14:10,11; 17:21). Now, in the 'Church Age', it's God's gathered people – as those abiding or remaining in God – who are to be the ones doing the Father's (greater) works on earth (John 14:12).

But to see how we can aspire to that, even as the Lord asked in prayer, let's go right back and begin at the very beginning – with the preaching of the Gospel. Allow me to share one of Jesus' most famous parables:

"The sower went out to sow his seed; and as he sowed, some fell beside the road, and it was trampled underfoot and the birds of the air ate it up. Other seed fell on rocky soil, and as soon as it grew up, it withered away, because it had no moisture. Other seed fell among the thorns; and the thorns grew up with it and choked it out. Other seed fell into the good soil, and grew up, and produced a crop a hundred times as great." As He said these things, He would call out, "He who has ears to hear, let him hear." His disciples began questioning Him as to what this parable meant.

And He said, "To you it has been granted to know the mysteries of the kingdom of God, but to the rest it is in parables, so that seeing they may not see, and hearing they may not understand. Now the parable is this: the seed is the word of God. Those beside the road are those who have heard; then the devil comes and takes away the word from their heart, so that they will not believe and be saved. Those on the rocky soil are those who, when they hear, receive the word with joy; and these have no firm root; they believe for a while, and in time of temptation fall away. The seed which fell among the thorns, these are the ones who have heard, and as they go on their way they are choked with worries and riches and pleasures of this life, and bring no fruit to maturity. But the seed in the good soil, these are the ones who have heard the word in an honest and good heart, and hold it fast, and bear fruit with perseverance." (Luke 8:5-15)

With some parables, there's a lot of debate over what they mean, but, thankfully, we can avoid that here because Jesus explains exactly what it means. He tells us that the outcome of preaching the word of God throughout the world (see Matthew 13:38) is like the varied result you get from sowing seed in a field. At times, there's no believing response because of the activity of the Devil. And, when there is a genuine response, the spiritual growth of those who become Christian believers can be stunted either because of difficulties or distractions. What the Lord is really looking for is represented by the type of ground where the seed falls and plants grow up and they, in turn, become very fruitful. This represents the case of sinners who hear God's word preached to them, and receive it in faith through the work of the Holy Spirit, so that they become Christian believers who go on to live productive Christian lives.

This is what the Lord wants, but the picture of individual plants isolated and scattered among other things in a field doesn't translate into Jesus' prayer vision of John 17, which asked for Christian believers to be gathered together visibly into one entity. Also in John 11:52, it was prophesied concerning Jesus' mission that He might also gather together into one the children of God who are scattered abroad.

Of course, Jesus' prayer was answered, and this prophecy came true. We can see exactly how Jesus' prayer was answered when we read on into Luke's sequel – the Bible book of the Acts – which is really the first history book of early Christian progress. Believers weren't left scattered in isolation, but the Apostles and evangelists, in their missionary enterprises, were careful to gather their converts – whom we're picturing as being like tender plants – into the New Testament churches of God, for example the local Church of God at Corinth.

Two Bible letters were later addressed to these people. In the first of the letters, in 1 Corinthians 3:9, Paul describes those converts, now settled into that local church, as '*God's cultivated land.*' Although the translations may not always show the difference, this is the word used for a farm or a garden – in other words, a place which has come under cultivation – the result of work which has been carried out by the divine gardener and those whom he uses.

So, let's step back again and see the full picture. Those growing Christian believers can be compared to 'seed in the good soil', having been planted as disciples by the Apostle Paul in the Church of God at Corinth. That is, they'd been transplanted by Paul into that church environment. The Lord had used Paul as his instrument to add these believers into this divine arrangement within 'his garden' where they might be gathered together with others.

We're seeing that individual plants in a field - symbolising individual Christians in the world - became collective arrays of plants in an enclosed garden – the Bible's way of describing them as being in a local church of God – having been added together by the gardener. Acts 2:47 clarifies for us that it was the Lord himself who added the first ever believers of the 'Church Age' to the very first church of God in Jerusalem. This is something that took place in space and time, and God involved humans – like Peter - as his agents back then. But essentially the Bible teaches us that it's the Lord who adds believers to the local church gathering. And notice, the Bible says the Lord adds those who are already individual believers to his own divine arrangement in the local church. This is not talking about unbelievers being set within the Church which is the Body of Christ (that which is comprised of all believers of the entire Church Age). No, the Lord adds believers into a local

Church of God, consistent with the clear biblical fact that God wants this particular, visible unity, rather than individualism.

We've seen this addition of believers happening 2,000 years ago at the very beginning of Christianity. However, this basic feature of Christianity which God so desires was anticipated even in the Old Testament times. God said: *"How good and how pleasant it is for brothers to dwell together in unity!"* (Psalm 133:1). In other words, even back then, God wasn't looking for a bunch of individualists but rather for a team, who, when gathered together, would be his people, displaying the unity that so pleases a God who himself exists as a perfect unity of three persons within the Godhead.

God is not looking for individually ambitious Christians, but he's looking for a people unitedly serving him in a visible togetherness that is, in itself, a witness to the world. The picture begins with a field having seed scattered on it, representing God's Word being preached in the world. Following God's sovereign plan, here and there, and scattered all over, there are individual responses to the Gospel. The resulting 'plants' are then to align themselves with God's desire for them to be added together with other believers, serving him faithfully according to his Word.

This is God's way, the way of unity, but an important question for us all to answer is: will it be God's way or our way in our lives? God's declared attitude towards self-will (1 Samuel 15:23) was shown once for all in the example of Saul when he chose to go his own way. Rather than doing what God had asked - instead of complying fully with God's instructions - Saul arrogantly thought he'd managed to come up with an even better idea, and then tried to defend it on the basis of it being a way to worship God! God denounced this as rebellion – read it for yourself later in First Samuel chapter 15 and verse 23.

So, we really do need to be sure that we're following God's intended way, as per his instructions in the Bible. We can be sure of doing that by following the highly instructive example of those very first Christians. And how do we find God's way? In Matthew 28:20, we have the Lord's Commandments: to go and make disciples, baptizing and teaching them to observe faithfully all of the Lord's commands – all of which are now found written in his New Testament Word. When the Apostles put this directly into practice two thousand years ago, as we find described in Acts 2:42, these commands then became known as the Apostles' Teaching, and are even later described in the short letter by Jude (v.3) as 'the Faith' – meaning the body of doctrine.

To be planted together in God's garden, if we follow the appealing picture language of the New Testament, individual plants - or Christians in other words - need to first set aside their own will, and allow themselves to be added together within the designed unity of God's arrangement – exactly as you would see plants arranged in a well-designed garden – and this garden is one that God himself can enjoy, fragrant with the obedience of Christian disciples following the way of his Son!

CHAPTER TWO: WHAT IS A 'CHURCH'?

We've previously shown that God's desire is for Christians to be gathered together and to serve him together. This was demonstrated right from the start of Christianity with the first Christians believing and practising a shared teaching known as 'the Apostles' teaching' (Acts 2:42). We now want to analyse various gatherings of people in the New Testament of the Bible which are referred to as 'churches' – so that we can understand what a church really is when it's stripped right down to the essentials.

In other words, we're asking: 'What is a church?' The very same New Testament Greek word for church actually refers to six quite different things in the New Testament. Let's find out what they are. We begin in the Bible Book of Acts, in chapter 19. The scene is set in Ephesus. Paul's preaching there had produced a downturn in business for the makers of pagan shrines. Reacting to that, the craftsmen, such as silversmiths, all grouped together, in united opposition against Paul and his preacher companions. Dr. Luke's report says: *"...some were shouting one thing and some another, for the assembly was in confusion and the majority did not know for what reason they had come together."* (Acts 19:32)

The word 'assembly' there is the same word in fact which in other places is translated as 'church.' Here, obviously, in context, it's being used to describe something like an unruly first-ever Trades Union Congress – a gathering of tradesmen called out to assemble in protest against the Christian message which seemed to be bad for their business!

We'll stay in the Book of Acts for our second reference. It's found in Acts 7:38, and there we read of how Stephen, the first Christian martyr, described Moses to the Jews as ... *"the one who was in the congregation in the wilderness together with the angel who was speaking to him on Mount Sinai, and who was with our fathers; and he received living oracles to pass on to you."* So, in his historical overview of Israel's Old Testament history, Stephen refers to *'the congregation in the wilderness.'* That word 'congregation' is again a translation of the same word usually translated as 'church'. And what was this congregation in the desert? It was the encampment of the children of Israel, of course, as they travelled through the desert and onward to the land God had promised them.

Our next example is found in Matthew's Gospel, in chapter 16, where we find Jesus asking his disciples: "But who do you say that I am?" Simon Peter answered, *"You are the Christ, the Son of the living God." And Jesus said to him, "Blessed are you, Simon Barjona, because flesh and blood did not reveal this to you, but My Father who is in heaven. I also say to you that you are Peter, and upon this rock I will build My church; and the gates of Hades will not overpower it."* (Matthew 16:15-18)

All who profess faith like Peter, are built into what is spoken of here as Christ's church. But this is no institution or denomination on earth. This is the church, biblically – and quite metaphorically – known as Christ's Body (Ephesians 1:23), into which all Christian believers of the present age have been incorporated irrespective of whether they're now dead or alive. We'll have more to say about this later.

But next is 1 Corinthians 1:2 where we read: *"To the church of God which is at Corinth, to those who have been sanctified in Christ Jesus, saints by calling, with all who in every place call on the name of our Lord Jesus Christ, their Lord and ours."* This use of the word 'church' is the most obvious one we've encountered so far. It's fully described as the church of God at Corinth, so it was the local group of Christian disciples based in that locality, who were continuing to be faithful to the things which the Apostle Paul had taught them before he moved away from that area.

By contrast, the following use of the word 'church' in 1 Timothy 3:15 needs just a little more care. This is Paul's first Bible letter to Timothy, and he says, *"I am writing these things to you, hoping to come to you before long; but in case I am delayed, I write so that you will know how one ought to conduct himself in the household of God, which is the church of the living God, the pillar and support of the truth."* (1 Timothy 3:14-15)

The Bible text here explains this church of the living God as being the household of God. This is something in which behaviour counts (as we see from the reference about conduct) and the reading here (check for yourself) has just been preceded by a discussion regarding potential candidates for the church offices of deacon and elder. When the Bible uses the descriptor 'household' or 'house' of God, as can be seen from other instances where it occurs (the Greek Word 'oikos' cannot mean 'family' here), it's speaking about something wider than just the local Church of God which we encountered earlier. It is, in fact, as Ephesians 2:20-21 shows, the fitly framing of all the local churches together so that they are seen to form one overall temple in the eyes of God. In other words, this use of 'church', in parallel with the term 'the household of God', relates to the New Testament people of God as a whole as they were found in all their different church locations.

So, finally, we come to Hebrews 12:23. This is a most interesting verse. We'll read the one before it, and the one after it also:

"But you have come to Mount Zion and to the city of the living God, the heavenly Jerusalem, and to myriads of angels, to the general

assembly and church of the firstborn who are enrolled in heaven, and to God, the Judge of all, and to the spirits of the righteous made perfect, and to Jesus, the mediator of a new covenant, and to the sprinkled blood, which speaks better than the blood of Abel." (Hebrews 12:22-24)

No prizes for guessing that this is a heavenly scene that's being described! And the close proximity of the mention of angels leads me to conclude that the 'church' mentioned which is more literally 'the church of the firstborn ones' is, in fact, a reference to some company of angels. These 'firstborn ones' would appear to be angelic 'beings of the first rank', judging by the cascading references to myriads of angels, the general assembly, and then this reference to a company or gathering of firstborn ones.

It's best not to be dogmatic, but if what I've presented is indeed the case, then we've now looked at a total of six different Bible applications of this same word, the one generally translated as 'church' in the New Testament. It's the Greek word 'ekklesia' and is commonly taken to describe those of whom it can in some way be said that they're 'called out and called together'. Even if we don't rely on justifying that meaning from the two component parts of this word, that clearly is the meaning when we review the various applications of it which we've been studying. For, we've seen tradesmen, Old Testament Jews, sinners, Christian disciples and angels as those who were called-out and gathered together to form each of the particular churches in question.

So, if we're asked which one of the following is the proper description of a church: a building; an organization; and a collection of people, I hope we'd all agree – irrespective of any modern usage – that the actual biblical definition of church has to be that of a collection of people.

Well, having looked at six different things the same word 'church' is applied to in the New Testament, we'd have to say that the two types of 'church' referred to most frequently by far in the New Testament are: the church which is Christ's body; and the churches of God. The first application is single and unique; whereas the latter is plural. That alone is sufficient to show that the designation 'the church of God' cannot possibly be an alternative title for 'the church which is Christ's body.' These are not the same churches at all.

However, in 1 Corinthians 12:27, the Apostle Paul does tell the local Church of God at Corinth that it is the Body of Christ in character. Those Christians at Corinth were not the whole Body of Christ, of course, for there were Christian believers existing elsewhere at that time, for example in the local Church of God at Jerusalem. As we said: there were many local churches of God; but only one Church which is Christ's Body. It's vital to distinguish between these, because churches of God, fitted together to become God's earthly temple, are said to be capable of being destroyed (1 Corinthians 3:16-17) – through such means as corrupt teaching; but on the other hand, the Church which is Christ's Body can never be destroyed (Matthew 16:16,18) The Lord stated unequivocally that the gates of Hades cannot prevail against it.

And another thing, believers, sadly, may be put away or dis-fellowshipped from a local church (1 Corinthians 5:13), but no true believer on Christ can ever be dismembered from the Body (John 10:28). Local churches have overseers and deacons; but in the Body, Christ is the Head. The underlying reality of the relationship between the Body and each local representation of it within a church of God must be acknowledged; while we appreciate that these things are not one and the same as such.

In order for local churches of God to appropriately express the glorious and eternal union of believers in the Body of Christ, it has to be that these local churches are all integrated into an overall unity – one facilitated by the governance of a fellowship of elders. How could earthly disagreement in doctrine and conduct ever be a worthy representation of the spiritual reality of the Body of Christ? This should give us food for thought as we look around on today's denominational chaos. How God longs for earthly unity to mirror spiritual reality!

CHAPTER THREE: THE FIRST LOCAL NEW TESTAMENT CHURCH

We've been looking at God's desire for Christians to be together, and we've also explored the Bible meaning of the word 'church'. The first local church of God to which we're introduced in the New Testament has its origin in the second chapter of the Bible book of Acts. Verses towards the end of that chapter, Acts 2:41-42, describe the result of the first gospel message. It was preached by the Apostle Peter to Jews who had travelled to Jerusalem for the Jewish (Old Testament) celebration of Pentecost. This was ten days after the ascension of the Lord Jesus Christ as it's recorded for us in chapter one of Acts. This particular day of Pentecost was to be the start of a new era, with the recorded beginnings of both 'the Church the body of Christ' and its first expression in a local church of God – which was to be in Jerusalem, the cradle of Christianity. We've previously seen the definitions and the distinction between these churches; and so now we want to move on to explore more fully the origin of that first local church of God at Jerusalem. Let's look closely at those verses we've highlighted:

"So then, those who had received his word were baptized; and that day there were added about three thousand souls. They were continually devoting themselves to the apostles' teaching and to [the] fellowship, to the breaking of bread and to [the] prayer[s]." (Acts 2:41-42)

There are seven particular actions contained in those two verses. Some of them describe things which happened once, but others relate to activities which were ongoing. The list is conveniently split into the two verses, 41 and 42. Verse 41 lists those actions which happened once: *"So then, those who had received his word were baptized; and that day there were added about three thousand souls."* (Acts 2:41)

It should also be said that these were things which were done individually by each of the believers – either done by them or something which was done to them. But, in any case, each of these first three actions was personal. By contrast, when we come to verse 42 and read: *"They were continually devoting themselves to the apostles' teaching and to [the] fellowship, to the breaking of bread and to [the] prayer[s] ..."*

The language makes it very clear that we're dealing here with repeated actions in each case – and what's more, actions which were carried out with others, having moved from the personal realm into the corporate. The words 'continually' and 'they' serve to make that obvious.

But now let's take a look at each of these seven actions, one by one, beginning with salvation – that is, the forgiveness of sins – which is the meaning of the wording *'received his word'* which is found in v.41. The Apostle Peter had preached the word or the message, as we have it summarized in the earlier verses of Acts chapter 2. The life, death and resurrection of Jesus of Nazareth had been preached, and the call given for a believing response – one evidenced by true repentance. To receive the word or the message meant to receive the one who was preached in that message, and that, of course, was Christ.

Peter, like Paul later, preached Christ, and him crucified. So, this receiving of the Word of Christ here agrees also with what John said in the opening of his Gospel, in John 1:12, when he spoke about receiving Christ, that is, by believing on his name, with the certain result of becoming a child of God through faith alone. When anyone responds like this he or she is born again, forgiven of all sins, and becomes the possessor of eternal life, all in that same moment, and sealed and assured through the Holy Spirit who's given to live in them from that time forward (Ephesians 1:13-14).

The second action listed in Acts 2:41-42 is baptism. As a general rule, when the New Testament mentions 'baptism', if it doesn't qualify the word, then it's water baptism which is intended. So, here we have it that: after they received the word, they were baptized. The meaning of the word 'baptized' is simply 'dipped' (Acts 8:38). After professing Christ as their personal saviour, these people were dipped in water. Why? What's the significance of this? Well, Romans 6:4-5 explains that this is a symbolic act on the part of the Christian believer. The act of going in, and then under, and finally coming back up out of the water dramatically represents death, burial and resurrection. The believer is, in this way, identifying himself or herself with Jesus in his death. It's an act which recognizes that his death was, in reality, our death; and so we're testifying publicly to others that we're now to be viewed as new people with new life in the one who rose victoriously from the dead. This baptism which we read about in the New Testament – for example in Romans chapter 6 verse 4 which speaks about 'burial in water' – was baptism performed by immersion.

Believer's baptism is a public act by which we identify ourselves with what took place at the cross where Jesus died. And as a practical result, we aim to live now in a new way as a follower of Jesus. The old ways of the old life are to be left behind. Clearly, this is only meaningful for someone who has already received salvation prior to water baptism – which was definitely the order of events set out in Acts 2:41. You see, it takes a new person to commit to living a new life under new management – living no longer for ourselves, but for our Lord.

It was Jesus who told his Apostles to go into the world and make disciples whom they were to baptize (Matthew 28:20). It became part of the Apostles' teaching (Acts 10:48), a requirement of biblical Christianity. And so, down to this day, this is a command we keep because we love the Lord who gave the command (John 14:15), and we do this to go public with the demonstration of our love for our Saviour. Jesus' original command, at the end of Matthew 28, described baptism as being performed in the name of the Father, Son and Holy Spirit. Notice it's the singular name of the triune God. Sometimes the New Testament records believers being baptized in the name of the Lord Jesus. But, of course, it would be perverse to take this as some kind of self-contradictory denial of the reality of the trinity. On the contrary, it reinforces the point that Matthew reports Jesus himself originally talking in terms of the singular name which represents all three persons of the Godhead.

But, we now need to ask: 'What happened to the newly-baptized believers at Pentecost?' Next in the list of Acts 2:41 is the act of being 'added' which makes a baptized disciple a part of the church of God in a particular city and so part of the Fellowship of God's Son in overall terms (1 Corinthians 1:9; Acts 2:42). Although it's much less talked about compared to salvation and baptism, we're surely not entitled to dispense with the fact that those who were baptised were 'added' (Acts 2:41,47; 5:14; 11:24). In its original context, we see this as always to do with baptized believers being joined to an existing group of local disciples.

Back in the nineteenth century, Christian believers debated the significance of 'added' and the connected issue of who should be admitted to participate at the 'Lord's table'. At that point in history, the thrilling, biblical teaching about the Church which is

Christ's Body (Ephesians 1:22, 23) had been freshly re-discovered. This brought with it a very natural desire to express the unity of 'the body' in the simple ordinance of the breaking of the bread, shorn of all ritual and transcending previous denominational barriers. As the movement spawned by this discovery matured, people began to differentiate between the unity of 'the body' and its various local expressions. As more consideration came to be given to these local expressions of Christ's Body, a sense of responsibility began to develop surrounding those who were considered eligible to be communicants at the Lord's Table in these local settings.

Debate took place between those who, by emphasizing the 'unity of the body', championed 'full fellowship' by all professing 'common life in Christ'; and those who, by emphasizing responsible local expressions of 'the body', insisted upon a more restricted or reserved circle of fellowship which considered a potential communicant's beliefs and behaviours. Achieving consistency in these matters was proving difficult. A decisive turning point in the debate arrived when it was seen just what people were added to, in the New Testament. Were sinners added to the 'body of Christ'? Or were believers added to its local expression? From verses such as those already referred to in Acts 2 & 5, those believers who historically in the nineteenth century came to form 'The Churches of God' understood it to be the latter: those who were added were already believers – members of 'the body' being added to its local expressions.

What's more, the Bible impressively teaches us that it's the Lord who adds believers to himself, by adding them to those disciples of his who are already called out and gathered together in the locality in question – in whichever town or city that may be (cf. Acts 1:12-15). Local church elders, appointed in each locality where there is a church of God (Acts 14:23; Titus 1:5), have the responsibility to discern when this is happening and to publicly recognize it on behalf of the church. Practically this will happen when they process a new applicant's desire to join the local church fellowship. Having satisfied themselves that the applicant is a baptised believer, they then recommend that the church receives such a person, who's then welcomed as a participant if there are no valid reasons offered by any as to why this should not happen.

"But," I hear you say, "you're reading more into these verses than is actually there. It's simply a way of saying that the Christian community was growing." Let's check that out. A helpful indication of the significance of any original biblical term comes from seeing how it was used in the surrounding Greek and Roman world of that time. Now, when the New Testament says believers were 'added', the sense was something like 'they went over from one party to another'. The Greek writers made use of this verb to describe the act by which towns, cities, or provinces changed their masters, and put themselves under another government. So, for example, the three thousand persons mentioned in Acts 2:41 left the side or party of the scribes and Pharisees, and put themselves under the teaching of the apostles and so under the lordship of Christ. They now unitedly professed the Christian doctrine ('the Faith'), having turned away from previously held erroneous teaching, perhaps that typical of the scribes and Pharisees. So this term had a clear theological significance: its use showed a definite, deliberate realigning under Christ's lordship. Growth, certainly, but of a specific type.

These verses, Acts 2:41-42, tell us that the first Christian believers 'continued steadfastly' in: *the apostles' teaching*; *the fellowship* (see 1 Corinthians 1:9 Revised Version); *the breaking of the bread* (see 1 Corinthians 11:18-29); and *the (church) prayers* (see Acts 12:5).

It's perhaps worth commenting first of all on what is meant by the phrase *'to continue steadfastly.'* The idea is something like 'being earnest towards a thing', or 'persevering diligently' with it. We might say they 'stuck at' *'the apostles' teaching'*; *'the fellowship'*; *'the breaking of the bread'*; and *'the* (church) *prayers'*. If we can catch anything of the original sense, it might be true to say they 'persisted obstinately' in these things. If that today suggests a negative connotation, then perhaps 'adhering firmly' is better.

It's interesting that the same word appears in Mark's Gospel chapter 3, verse 9, in one of the recorded instances of Jesus preaching and teaching by the seashore. There was concern expressed that the crowd of listeners might crush in around Jesus, so out of thoughtfulness, provision was made *'that a little boat should wait on him.'* It's this same word meaning 'continue steadfastly' that's used there. The boat was to keep close (Greek: proskartereo) to the shore in constant readiness and to track along the shoreline as Jesus himself moved. Whether he needed it or not, we're not told, but it was there anyway, always ready.

Now, we can't necessarily force the same translation in another context, but it may suggest another angle to think around: namely that these first believers stayed close to the Lord, moving with him in accordance with his will, and with a constant readiness to wait on him so as to serve him in the four ways described as *'the apostles' teaching'*; *'the fellowship'*; *'the breaking of the bread'*; and *'the* (church) *prayers'*. And we see clearly that theirs was a learning that lived; a fellowship that functioned, a worship that warmed and a praying that powered all their service for the Lord!

So, having dealt previously with the three personal actions listed in Acts 2:41, we now want to examine in some more detail the remainder of the list which describes continuing involvement by the whole local church. For they were to continue steadfastly in:

'the apostles' teaching'; 'the fellowship'; 'the breaking of the bread'; and 'the (church) *prayers'.*

At this point, perhaps we can begin to appreciate that, in some sense, this list in Acts 2:41-42 has got to be viewed as a protective setting. Let me explain what I mean by that. For a start, it's quite inappropriate – as you will doubtless agree – that a non-believer should participate in the breaking of the bread at the Lord's table, for the Acts 2 verses clearly state that 'receiving the word' must precede everything else in the list, in order to make what follows meaningful.

And then, notice also, if you will, that these verses in Acts 2 also mention baptism in sequence prior to any participation in the Breaking of the Bread or 'holy communion' as some refer to it. How right it is that there should be acknowledgement of the lordship of Christ before there's any participation at the Lord's table. And then, through addition, and so now as an added part of a biblical church of God, a believer has then the privilege and responsibility to break bread.

Now, the Breaking of the Bread in the New Testament is always (though sometimes implicitly so) presented as a corporate act of those who are biblically constituted a church of God in a given locality (e.g. 1 Corinthians 1:2; Acts 20:7). Notice how the apostle Paul sets the instruction *"This do ... in remembrance of Me"* (1 Corinthians 11:25; cf. Luke 22:19-20) in the context of *"When you come together 'in church'..."* (1 Corinthians 11:18).

It's also quite telling when, in the adjacent verses there, he speaks against those who were abusing the privilege of participation in the Breaking of the Bread by accusing them of 'despising the Church of God'. What that does is underline the strength of connection between the two, and shows pretty conclusively where the Breaking of the Bread rightly belongs: as one of the four continual functions of a biblical church of God, one that's modelled on the pattern of Acts 2.

Remember, we're emphasizing how the four things listed in Acts 2:42 were corporate items: things which they did together with each other. The fact that they were a community who did those things is underlined in the fact that it says they continued steadfastly in the fellowship. The community (as a movement empowered by God's Spirit) began in Acts 2 – and from verses 44-47 we get a genuine sense of the character of its community life from reading about the actions of those who belonged to it ...

"Out of love, they provided for each other's practical needs: All those who had believed were together and had all things in common ... sharing them with all, as anyone might have need. Day by day continuing with one mind ... taking their meals together with gladness and sincerity of heart, praising God."

It's said of them that they were 'together' (Greek: 'epi to auto'). These Greek words signify either, at one time (Acts 3:1); or in one place (Acts 2:1); or in one thing. The last of these three senses seems the most fitting here; for it's hardly likely that the believers, who were then about three thousand in number, besides the 120 (Acts 1:15), were able to all meet at one time in one place in Jerusalem.

What was it that gave them this sense of togetherness and quality of fellowship? It had been made possible by the descent of the Holy Spirit as recorded earlier in Acts chapter 2. There's no mention of 'koinonia' or fellowship in the New Testament before that. This was a unity of the Spirit in arriving at what the Bible calls 'the fellowship' as something belonging to the Lord Jesus Christ. Sometimes, today, we relegate the word 'fellowship' to mean enjoying a cup of coffee with a Christian friend. But biblically, fellowship meant a joint participation in things of mutual interest – and that interest which they shared in common was something produced in them by the Holy Spirit. There are various ways in which 1 Corinthians 1:9 has been translated, but it was describing a local church exactly like this one, and one learned commentator says the words here: "[the] fellowship of the son of [God] ... may ... reflect the idea of the fellowship of believers that has been formed in his Son" (The First Epistle to the Corinthians, G.D. Fee, NICNT, Eerdmans, 1987). Yes, that's it: a fellowship of believers owned by the Lord.

Now factor in 1 Corinthians 1:2 – *"To the church of God which is at Corinth ... with all who in every place call on the name of our Lord Jesus Christ, their Lord and ours"* – and we arrive at: ... a definite community of born-again disciples, all baptized by immersion in water, all added locally to church of God fellowship, all serving according to one pattern of teaching in every place, all maintained under a fellowship of elders while being separated to God.

What was true in the church fellowship at Jerusalem was true equally of the fellowship of churches. And so a people formed in New Testament times who mirrored God's people in the Old Testament. There was a difference, however: in the Old Testament, God's people were physically together in one location; now that was no longer true physically. Instead, here was what Jesus had looked forward to when speaking with the woman at Sychar's well in John 4, when he'd said, *"Neither in this mountain nor in Jerusalem ..."* No, physical locations would no longer be of the essence, but would be replaced with a spiritual gathering of disciples of Christ; no longer a physical gathering in any one place – but a single people who, although in different places geographically, were spiritually united together 'on the same page' – like the original community at Jerusalem in Acts 2.

All God's revealed purposes in the past, through Abraham to Moses and beyond, were centred on the establishment of a community of believers who would come together in unity of heart and purpose – in close relationship not only with each other, but also with God – so close in fact that God repeatedly referred to them as 'My people' in the Old Testament. It's not in the least bit surprising, then, to find that same value and importance given to the idea of 'community' in the New Testament, amongst those who believed in the Lord Jesus Christ.

If we're to follow their example, there's no room for a 'lowest common denominator' approach today. Was it not our Lord's expressed desire for his followers *"that they may all be one"* (John 17:20-23)? Unity like this can only be reached through a sincere commitment on our part to carefully follow the teaching pattern the Lord laid down in his Word (Romans 6:17; 2 Timothy 1:13). The Apostolic teaching, which Paul transmitted to Timothy, was no mere outline or rough sketch of truth. What Paul had handed to Timothy for safe-keeping was *'the pattern of... sound words.'* The word 'pattern' means a mould or model, so something definite and precise. One Bible version in fact translates it as 'the standard', as in the standard teaching in all the then churches of God. And that's exactly what it was. For Paul taught the same thing wherever he went – he says *'as I teach everywhere in every church'* (see 1 Corinthians 4:17; 7:17).

Among their gatherings were times when they came together to pray. *'Pray without ceasing'* (1 Thessalonians 5:17), Paul says. Not non-stop prayer, of course, for that would be impossible. The same word long ago was used to describe a person's hacking cough. They weren't coughing non-stop, but if ever you were in that person's company you'd be left in no doubt that they had a cough that was persistent. So we, as Christian believers, are commanded to develop a regular habit of prayer – church prayer as well as a personal prayer life (Acts 4;12).

CHAPTER FOUR: THE BROADER PICTURE: THE FIRST MENTION OF GOD'S HOUSE

We've already seen from our Bibles that God doesn't want individual Christians to be isolated, nor to be gathered together to do as they please, but rather to be gathered together based on their obedience to his teaching – which was, of course, first given by the Lord Jesus himself.

Our aim now is to move on to see God's principle of unity explored a stage further. We want to build up the broader New Testament picture of the spiritual house of God on earth consisting, as it did in New Testament times, of all of those churches of God – just like the one at Jerusalem – but including all those found in the other locations we encounter throughout the various towns and cities and indeed countries mentioned in the New Testament. Because even churches of God themselves were never intended by God to be independent or autonomous. Rather, they form overall a united testimony on earth because they have consistent doctrine and practice throughout. This integrated pattern was established back in Old Testament times, as we'll now see when we look back at the first indications God ever gave to the human race about such a thing as his longing to live with us in what he himself calls 'his house' on this earth.

The first mention of a thing in the Bible is generally considered important; so much so that some have formulated it as 'the law of first mention'. Well, the first mention of a house of God on this earth is found in Genesis 28 which we should now read:

"Then Jacob departed from Beersheba and went toward Haran. He came to a certain place and spent the night there, because the sun had set; and he took one of the stones of the place and put it under his head, and lay down in that place. He had a dream, and behold, a ladder was set on the earth with its top reaching to heaven; and behold, the angels of God were ascending and descending on it. And behold, the LORD stood above it and said, "I am the LORD, the God of your father Abraham and the God of Isaac; the land on which you lie, I will give it to you and to your descendants. Your descendants will also be like the dust of the earth, and you will spread out to the west and to the east and to the north and to the south; and in you and in your descendants shall all the families of the earth be blessed. Behold, I am with you and will keep you wherever you go, and will bring you back to this land; for I will not leave you until I have done what I have promised you."

Then Jacob awoke from his sleep and said, "Surely the LORD is in this place, and I did not know it." He was afraid and said, "How awesome is this place! This is none other than the house of God, and this is the gate of heaven." So Jacob rose early in the morning, and took the stone that he had put under his head and set it up as a pillar and poured oil on its top. He called the name of that place Bethel; however, previously the name of the city had been Luz. Then Jacob made a vow, saying, "If God will be with me and will keep me on this journey that I take, and will give me food to eat and garments to wear, and I return to my father's house in safety, then the LORD will be my God. This stone, which I have set up as a pillar, will be God's house, and of all that You give me I will surely give a tenth to You."
(Genesis 28:10-22)

Perhaps some of the background leading up to this incident would be helpful at this stage. This is the man Jacob who was born a split-second after his twin brother, Esau. He actually emerged literally on the heels of his brother. He was holding his brother by the heel, a posture which would prove to be rather telling, and indeed it explains the meaning of the name given to him as 'the one who takes by the heel.' In life, whatever Esau had, Jacob wanted. In those ancient times, the desirable things belonging to Esau were what were known as the birthright and the blessing. These things both belonged to the son who was born first. He received a double portion of the father's inheritance and was also given his father's blessing.

However, Jacob's mother, Rebekah, during a difficult pregnancy, had been told by God that – contrary to convention – her younger son would in fact become the greater of the two, as the one chosen by God. Jacob had doubtless learned this information from his mother, and with her help, he tried his best to make it happen. By a combination of taking unfair advantage and by telling outright lies, Jacob obtained both the birthright and the blessing which would normally have been his brother's. Of course, this made Esau very angry, and it was no longer safe for Jacob to remain at home.

He set out on a long journey, running away to the place where his mother's relatives lived. It would be twenty years before he ever returned to face his brother again. We can only wonder at his state of mind as he tried to put as many miles as possible between himself and home. Was he guilt-ridden, not proud of what he'd done, or was he smugly satisfied? Or some combination of all three? He was certainly exhausted, that's for sure: tired enough to lie down on the ground and use a stone for his pillow. And when he slept, he dreamed.

He dreamt of a ladder reaching up from that place where he now was, and reaching into heaven itself. There were angels going up and down on it, and the Lord himself stood above it and was now speaking to him as he had spoken to Jacob's father and to his grandfather, Abraham. God was confirming his previous plans, but now doing it personally with Jacob. There was no censure or rebuke for what Jacob had done, although the means Jacob had used to align himself with God's purpose couldn't possibly have pleased the Lord.

Well, Jacob awoke, startled, declaring with reverence that that very place must be God's house – which was the name he now gave to it – and announced that this was the gate of heaven. I suppose it's possible he then went back to sleep, but when he rose early in the morning, he set up his stone pillow as a memorial stone and ceremonially anointed it with oil. So, this stone went from being a pillow to becoming a pillar. And there Jacob vowed or pledged his commitment to God – the first time we hear this from Jacob – and he promised to honour God with his wealth.

Suppose at this point we use our imagination and imagine that along comes a man with a camel passing by the place where Jacob now was, previously known as Luz. Jacob is still very excited and tells the stranger that this very place is God's house. How do we think the traveller would react? He'd look around at the unremarkable tract of ground with its few scattered stones, and say: "Where?" Jacob would reply, "Right here, in this place where I slept last night. This is God's house. I've had it revealed to me in a dream." Probably, the stranger would take another look around, again seeing nothing – for truthfully there was nothing to see – and, comparing this with his past acquaintance with religious sites, would shake his head dismissively, and lead his camel away, while muttering under his breath, "That's one crazy guy!"

After a moment's thought, Jacob might have said, "I should have expected that reaction. After all, there's nothing to see here: no stunning architecture; no choirs of angels; no sign in the sky." But then he thinks, "But that changes nothing for me, because I've received God's word about this, conveyed in a dream, and I know it to be true, and so from now on this place will be called Bethel, meaning the house of God."

And it's much the same in this present Church Age, although different in some respects, as we'll see. But, it's still easy for people to overlook God's house on earth because it's not what they imagine it should be like. More of that later on, in our study.

But as we now examine more closely Jacob's worshipful response, we see how he felt that respect for God was due in this place of revelation – a place where the Lord had been shown to be exalted in authority. We see, too, that remembrance of what had taken place would be necessary, marked by the place being set apart as different from any other place by use of the pillar and oil. What's more, the revelation he had received there was affirmed by Jacob by his naming of the place in full agreement with what had been shown to him. And to all these things, Jacob added his commitment, and a promise to give something back to God.

These are the striking features of God's house, as presented to us in the story of Jacob, where we've the first mention of the house of God in the whole of the Bible. I say the whole of the Bible, for the theme of God's house on earth runs throughout the Bible and those same features we've noted here in Genesis chapter 28 always accompany it. What were they again? Well, there was respect for God in that revealed place; remembrance, too, at that place of God's choice; and a recognition that he needed to set apart what God himself had set apart; together with a pledge of commitment to worship there.

CHAPTER FIVE: INSTRUCTIVE SYMBOLISM FROM THE TIME OF MOSES

The next Bible character we associate with the developing picture of God's house is Moses. This is the Moses who later led Jacob's descendants out of slavery in Egypt and to the border of the land God had promised to give them. En route, and at God's very specific instruction, Moses built what was then known as the Tabernacle. If you need to remind yourself of the details of this special tent in which God lived at that time among all his people's tents, then turn to the book of Exodus, for God devotes no less than the last fifteen chapters of that book to it. That fact alone should grab our attention. The creation of this entire and magnificent universe is dismissed in a few words in Genesis chapter one, but in remarkable contrast, this small, temporary and portable structure, known as the Tabernacle, has all this space devoted to it in God's Word. And the New Testament returns our thoughts to it in the letter to the Hebrews where the Spirit-led writer employs these historical things as object lessons which are of vital importance to our present day discipleship.

This further progression of God's desire to live among men and women on this earth had been waiting until such time as God had a people who had passed through experiences later known biblically as redemption, baptism, and separation from others. These were necessary so that they could become a people who would obey God's teachings, and also worship and serve God at his house.

It will be helpful to summarize the developing Old Testament story of God's house – specifically in these terms - by looking back on them from the New Testament. In 1 Corinthians 5:7, we find Jesus Christ described as *'our Passover* (lamb).' This is a reference back to the time of Moses when God delivered his ancient people Israel out of slavery to Pharaoh in Egypt. At that time, he secured their release from a reluctant Pharaoh after troubling the land of Egypt with ten plagues which were his judgements. The last of these was the slaying of all firstborn sons. All, that is, except for those in whose homes the doorways had been treated with the blood of a sacrificed lamb. As promised, God 'passed over' those Israelite homes when he carried out this final judgement on Egypt with all its false gods. Then, in bitter grief, Pharaoh freed his slaves and sent the Israelites away. And that's how the Jews were delivered from slavery – they were saved by the blood of a lamb (one for each household) – known naturally enough as the 'Passover' lamb. Those lambs are used by God in the Bible as a major object lesson – one of the Bible's great prophetic 'types' or foreshadowings of the sacrifice of Christ on the cross for our deliverance from another slavery, this time from slavery to sin.

However, returning to the time of Moses, when Pharaoh realized he was now without free labour, he once again changed his mind about releasing the Israelite slaves. He pursued with his army, chasing after the departing Israelites who were now discovering that their way was blocked by the Red Sea, as it acted like a barrier in front of them. As hope for their means of escape faded, God commanded Moses to stretch his arm out over the Red Sea, holding out his staff. At this, the sea opened up so that the Israelites could pass over the dry sea-bed. When the pursuing Egyptians tried to follow, however, the walls of water collapsed, drowning them. And so the Israelites' new way of life began, a life that was to be one of walking with God. When the Apostle Paul, again in his first Bible letter to the Corinthians, refers to this sequel, he uses very interesting language: *"For I do not want you to be unaware, brethren, that our fathers were all under the cloud and all passed through the sea; and all were baptized into Moses in the cloud and in the sea ..."* (1 Corinthians 10:1-2)

Do you see how Paul, by the Spirit of God, relates their historic watershed experience in coming out of Egypt, to Christian believer's baptism today? And it's a very graphic picturing of baptism by total immersion in water, I'm sure you'll agree, for the Israelites who crossed the Red Sea, did so by passing between water on either side of them, and they also had the watery cloud above their heads. So, it's as if they were burying their old way of life, and identifying with their new leader, Moses, who was leading them to experience a new way of life for God. And that's a true fit for the meaning of our water baptism, as believers on Christ. For Paul adds in Romans chapter 6:

"Or do you not know that all of us who have been baptized into Christ Jesus have been baptized into His death? Therefore we have been buried with Him through baptism into death, so that as Christ was raised from the dead through the glory of the Father, so we too might walk in newness of life. For if we have become united with Him in the likeness of His death, certainly we shall also be in the likeness of His resurrection ..." (Romans 6:3-5)

Into, under and up out of the water again, as with the Israelites at the Red Sea: it's a complete picture of death, burial and resurrection, witnessing to all who watch our baptism that we're identifying with Christ in his death. It has the practical significance that we're promising to live no longer for sinful things, but for the Lord.

Then, after the Israelites moved on from the Rea Sea shore, they soon came to Mount Sinai, from where God thundered his 'Ten Commandments' (Exodus 20). This giving of the Law, soon to be known as the Law of Moses, was prefaced by God telling the people of Israel that if they would obey then they would be for him a special people, a holy nation, and a kingdom of priests (Exodus 19:5-6). Under Moses' leadership, the people replied in unison that *'all the LORD had spoken they would do and be obedient'* (Exodus 24:7). Now, with a redeemed, baptized and obedient people, the stage was finally set for God's desire among them – and his purpose through them – to be further realized. So, straightaway, in Exodus chapter 25, we read:

> *"Then the LORD spoke to Moses, saying, "Tell the sons of Israel to raise a contribution for Me; from every man whose heart moves him you shall raise My contribution. This is the contribution which you are to raise from them: gold, silver and bronze, blue, purple and scarlet material, fine linen, goat hair, rams' skins dyed red, porpoise skins, acacia wood, oil for lighting, spices for the anointing oil and for the fragrant incense, onyx stones and setting stones for the ephod and for the breastpiece. Let them construct a sanctuary for Me, that I may dwell among them. According to all that I am going to show you, as the pattern of the tabernacle and the pattern of all its furniture, just so you shall construct it."* (Exodus 25:1-9)

The sanctuary in question is, of course, the Tabernacle, as is obvious from the description of the materials, and the following chapters detailing how they were later used to construct that very special tent. We read there that the construction was all to be to God's pattern. There was no scope at all for human ingenuity. This was God's house, so it had to be to God's design.

In various ways, the biblical associations of these materials direct our thoughts to the person and work of Christ, the one who is *'son over God's house'* today. And if we aspire to make the claim to be God's spiritual house on earth today – a claim found in Hebrews 3:6 – then we should do our very best to reflect his character in how we live and how we attempt to adorn his teaching (even that of his apostles, see Acts 2:42).

CHAPTER SIX: THE IMPORTANCE OF DOING THINGS GOD'S WAY

Have you ever doubted the sovereignty of God – the fact that he's in control? The Philistines put the idea to the test. They were the Old Testament enemy of God's people and had captured the Ark of the Covenant when it had been wrongly removed from its sanctuary in God's house and taken into battle by the Israelites. The Israelites had lost all perspective at this point, and were treating this sacred box as if it were like the idol of one of the false gods of the surrounding nations. However, when the Philistines placed the captured Ark in the house of their god, Dagon, his image lay smashed before it in the morning. Wherever it visited throughout the five cities of the Philistine lords, disaster and mayhem followed. Finally, they held a committee meeting to decide to send the Ark back to the Israelites on a cart or wagon. But to make sure that everything that had happened to them since its arrival wasn't just some strange string of coincidences, they agreed to stack the odds against the Ark making it back.

They selected oxen that had never previously borne a yoke. In addition, the oxen had recently calved. Without guidance they were unlikely to head directly into Israelite territory. Natural instinct would be expected to draw them back to their calves. However, as it turned out, the oxen pulled the wagon with the Ark directly back to Israelite territory, to Bethshemesh in fact, confirming miraculously to the Philistines that the hand of God had been in all that had happened. (You can read the Bible narrative in 1 Samuel 4:1-11 & 5:1-7:1)

When the inhabitants of Bethshemesh saw the Ark returning, First Samuel chapter six tells us they rejoiced to see it. Bethshemesh was a Levite city and so the Ark of God would be especially meaningful to them. After that initial joy, we read that during the time while Saul was king, it was simply left in Kiriath Jearim. In First Chronicles 13:3 we read that Israel didn't seek out the Ark during all that time. It just didn't seem to figure in Saul's plans or thinking.

What a contrast with the king who succeeded him! David, his successor, was a man after God's own heart – in other words he cared for the things God cared for. When he came to the throne, after capturing Jerusalem, David made it a priority to fetch the Ark up from the 'fields of the woods' where Psalm 132 indicates it had lain throughout the reign of Saul. David's first move in removing the ark to Jerusalem, however, was to prove to be a false one (as recorded in 2 Samuel 6:3-7).

Perhaps influenced by what the Philistines had done, David also set the Ark on a wagon pulled by oxen. They hadn't gone far before the oxen stumbled and a man called Uzzah stuck out his hand to steady the Ark. For doing what had long ago been forbidden, even to the Levites – for touching the sacred chest that symbolized the presence of God – Uzzah was struck down dead by God. We don't know all that lay behind this. Uzzah was one of the family who had given shelter to the Ark. Perhaps familiarity had bred contempt, and it had come to be for him just an old box that stood in the corner of the house.

What we do know is that David caused the journey to be aborted, and the Ark was diverted into the house of a man called Obed-edom. David might be surprised, confused, displeased and disappointed - but two clear commands of God's Word had been broken. God had clearly said in Moses' time that not even the Levites were to touch the Ark. It was to be carried by staves or poles on their shoulders. Wagons could be used for transporting other Tabernacle objects, but not for the Ark of God.

But the strange thing is that the Philistines appeared to have got away with this. Surely the lesson for us is obvious: that the people of God – those to whom he has revealed his will – may not do as others do. Greater privilege and understanding brings greater responsibility.

David did learn his lesson and, after seeing that God had blessed the family of Obed-edom where the Ark was, First Chronicles 15 tells us how David assembled all Israel at Jerusalem to bring the Ark there. It would be carried this time by the Levites – which was now in agreement with God's written instructions of five hundred years earlier. You may ask, "Do details matter to God?" This incident has been recorded in the Bible to serve as our answer – a resounding 'yes' – details matter! God's actions then reveal what remains his attitude now. That story underlines for us the importance of following God's Word exactly and carefully – above all in things relating to God's house.

The Tabernacle – where the Ark was housed – was used by Israel in the wilderness and after they entered the land of Canaan. Later, it was replaced by a more permanent structure: the Temple. It was David who first wanted God to have a temple (2 Samuel 7:1-11), but it was Solomon, his son, who was instrumental in building it (2 Samuel 7:12,13; Acts 7:47).

Once again, it is instructive for us how this came about. Sometime after David had brought the Ark to Jerusalem, and after David was settled in his palace, he said to Nathan the prophet, *"Here I am, living in a house of cedar, while the ark of the covenant of the LORD is under a tent." Nathan replied to David, "Whatever you have in mind, do it, for God is with you."* (1 Chronicles 17:1-2 NIV).

David's concern was a very worthy one. He was moved by the homelessness of God on this earth! He saw with painful clarity how incongruous it was that he should have a nice place to live, when God had no place at all. But if you read further in that chapter – for we've only read the first two verses – we would find God corrects his prophet. It could never be that the house built for God would be the product of David's own mind – or any human mind. God's house, if it is to be God's house truly, must be to God's design, it must be exclusively from the mind of God, faithfully communicated to the builders, and acted upon with accuracy.

True enough, David later recounted what did eventually happen: *"All this,"* said David, *"the LORD made me understand in writing by His hand upon me, all the details of this pattern."* (1 Chronicles 28:19). Not only that, but David was not even allowed to be the builder. God told David that his son, Solomon, would be the one to build the Temple. It wouldn't be David, despite him being the one with the motivation, because he was a man of blood – probably not exclusively referring to all the wars he had engaged in, but possibly also referring to the blood of Uriah which he had spilled so as to obtain that man's wife.

And Solomon did indeed build God's house. It was a magnificent temple, constructed fully in compliance with God's building pattern which had been communicated by God to Solomon's father, David. And so we come to read in 1 Kings 6:7 (ESV), *"... When the house was built, it was with stone prepared at the quarry, so that neither hammer nor axe nor any tool of iron was heard in the house while it was being built."*

That's an interesting detail we find there about the actual construction process. All the stone was cut and prepared at the quarry before transportation to the actual temple site. Then, at the site, the stones were added together and built into the house.

I remember visiting this site at Jerusalem. The guide took us to a quarry that was underground, and explained that it was thought that stones from this quarry had found their place in Solomon's Temple. Since it was underground, the Bible verse could be satisfied that no sound was heard from the quarrying and shaping processes. As we exited the quarry, you could see over to what is believed to have been the place where the cross of Jesus stood. I enjoyed the thought then that Christian believers today are living stones quarried at Calvary, shaped by God, for a place in God's house. But more on that in the next chapter ...

So far, in our brief history of God's house down through the ages, we've observed how the desire God first expressed to Jacob was given effect to in the time of Moses in terms of the Tabernacle; and later in the time of Solomon in terms of the permanent temple structure located at Jerusalem. In overall terms, it's interesting, but sad, to see a feature of the human response to this great desire of God's heart. I'm referring to how the house of God in Old Testament times suffered a period of decline and dormancy and, only after this, was it restored.

There was the glorious beginning in the desert so graphically recounted in Exodus chapter 40 which proclaims repeatedly Moses' obedience, and emphasizes the glory of God crowning the completed Tabernacle house. A good beginning. Sadly, this was not maintained throughout the times of the Judges. There was revival in relation to this central theme of God's heart, as we saw during David's reign, leading to Solomon building the Temple. But then once again, in the process of time, decline set in. There was deterioration because of idolatry during the time of the kings of Israel and Judah, until it ceased to function with the captivity in Babylon. However, in the mercy of God, there was restoration – by a remnant (a fraction of the people), under the leadership of Ezra and Nehemiah, which was about five centuries before the coming of Christ.

CHAPTER SEVEN: A MAJOR TRANSITION

As we continue our brief history of God's house, we would now like to explore a key transition that began to be indicated during the life of the Lord Jesus Christ on earth. It was from that time that the physical house of God was transferred from the nation of Israel; and, after Christ's ascension back into heaven, was replaced with a spiritual house for disciples of all nationalities.

In his teaching, and particularly in his judgements against the religious leaders of that time, Jesus began to make this impending change very clear. For example, *"Jerusalem, Jerusalem, who kills the prophets and stones those who are sent to her! How often I wanted to gather your children together, the way a hen gathers her chicks under her wings, and you were unwilling. Behold, your house is being left to you desolate!"* (Matthew 23:37-38)

There's no doubt here that Jesus was referring to the Jerusalem Temple. The one that had been rebuilt by those Jews who, under Zerubbabel, Ezra and Nehemiah, had returned from exile to rebuild on the same basis as before at Jerusalem. By the time Jesus visited this Temple, it had been beautified by Herod the Great, although that had nothing at all to do with God's wishes or plans. And now Jesus was plainly saying that God was finished with that building. It would be left desolate of the divine presence. He would no longer honour or sanctify it by his presence. The Jews, through their religious leadership, had rejected Jesus as the Christ, so God was rejecting in turn their physical temple – and indeed, closing the chapter on his dealings with them – for a while, at least.

Then Jesus also began to disclose what God's future plans were, especially those plans surrounding his house on earth. It's been plain to us so far, I trust, that this idea of God living on earth among a chosen, obedient people, and their serving and worshiping him centred on that place of his residence, is shown to be a major or central part of God's mainstream purpose with his human creation, and so God wasn't likely going to abandon all notion of it now. It would be transformed, not terminated.

But what was it going to look like, going forward? In one of his parables, spoken against the Jewish leaders, Jesus sharpens things up as follows:

"And He began to speak to them in parables: "A man planted a vineyard and put a wall around it, and dug a vat under the wine press and built a tower, and rented it out to vine-growers and went on a journey. At the harvest time he sent a slave to the vine-growers, in order to receive some of the produce of the vineyard from the vine-growers. They took him, and beat him and sent him away empty-handed. Again he sent them another slave, and they wounded him in the head, and treated him shamefully. And he sent another, and that one they killed; and so with many others, beating some and killing others. He had one more to send, a beloved son; he sent him last of all to them, saying, 'They will respect my son.' But those vine-growers said to one another, 'This is the heir; come, let us kill him, and the inheritance will be ours!' They took him, and killed him and threw him out of the vineyard. What will the owner of the vineyard do? He will come and destroy the vine-growers, and will give the vineyard to others. Have you not even read this Scripture: The stone which the builders rejected, this became the chief corner stone; this came about from the LORD, and it is marvelous in our eyes?" (Mark 12:1-11)

From this, we get the clear sense that Jesus himself is the rejected stone about which he's talking – rejected, that is, by the Jewish religious nation-builders. The picture of a vineyard, ever since the time of Isaiah chapter 5, had been in vogue as a metaphor for Israel as God's kingdom on earth – one from which God expected such 'fruits' as righteousness, justice, faithfulness and obedience. Sadly, these had been in short supply throughout Israel's chequered history, and now their attitude towards the Christ whom God had sent, represented an all-time low. Judgement was inevitable. That judgement was the removal of 'kingdom status' from Israel, and a new beginning built around the same Christ figure whom they had rejected.

In Luke chapter 12, Jesus goes further, because here he's explaining to his faithful disciples, so he says: *"Do not be afraid, little flock, for your Father has chosen gladly to give you the kingdom"* (Luke 12:32).

So, that kingdom status that was being removed from Israel nationally, was being transferred to these followers of Jesus and those who would succeed them on the same basis.

This is indeed the language which the New Testament attributes to the early pioneers of the churches of God which started to form around the Mediterranean seaboard and hinterlands, beginning from Jerusalem, of course. It was there that some of the apostolic representatives of this new movement of God, proclaimed to the same opposing authorities: *"He is the stone which was rejected by you, the builders, but which became the chief corner stone"* (Acts 4:11).

They were still speaking of Jesus, of course, and using the same terminology that Jesus himself had used. Peter had been the spokesperson then, and later in the first Bible letter bearing his name which the Holy Spirit would cause to be inspired and so included in our Bibles, he wrote: *"For this is contained in Scripture: "Behold, I lay in Zion a choice stone, a precious corner stone, and he who believes in Him will not be disappointed." This precious value,* then, is for you who believe; but for those who disbelieve, "The stone which the builders rejected, this became the very corner stone" (1 Peter 2:6-7).

The consistency and persistency of this same metaphor of Jesus, as the most important stone in God's building, is very noticeable. But what was this building which was anticipated as the replacement house for God on earth? It was now no Tabernacle or Temple or cathedral or abbey or any artifice that was the result of human ingenuity. In fact, it wasn't a building at all – at least not in physical terms. We're introduced instead to a spiritual counterpart of what had previously existed in Old Testament times. If we look at an adjacent verse from 1 Peter 2, we'll understand how he is extending the metaphor about a stone to more people now than Jesus: *"And coming to Him as to a living stone which has been rejected by men, but is choice and precious in the sight of God, you also, as living stones, are being built up as a spiritual house for a holy priesthood, to offer up spiritual sacrifices acceptable to God through Jesus Christ"* (1 Peter 2:4-5).

So, what exactly is being said? What is this spiritual house made up of living stones? We don't have to look far, to see what fills the pages of the New Testament, as really the only candidate for what this could be. The living stones referred to those believers in the churches being established then by the apostles on their missionary journeys (of which the most famous are certainly those of Paul). Yet we shouldn't overlook missionary travel and work by lesser known men like Epaphras, whose work, as with that of others, led to church-plantings as churches of God spread even as far as Europe, in the account of the Acts of the Apostles.

This all fits. Earlier in this series of studies, we defined biblically what those churches of God actually were. And, later, we hope to explore their integration with each other – as sister churches – so that they really did form overall a single spiritual house for God or residence for him by his Spirit. But, for now, it's sufficient that we concentrate on this most significant change-point regarding God's long-term desire for a house on earth. Many people may dream of a second home these days, but this was something God meticulously planned for: that he should have a residence among his human creation, subject, of course, to them fulfilling his terms and conditions. For he is, after all, the holy God of heaven.

But in the New Testament we already see developing the same sad trend as was faithfully documented in the Old Testament. The story of God's house again repeats as one of beginning, followed by decline. But again, by God's grace, there was the opportunity for subsequent restoration. How wonderfully it began in Acts chapter 2 with the apostles, and how from that time of Pentecost they laboured under God to establish and maintain faithful New Testament churches of God in every place. But read Revelation chapters 2 and 3, and the Lord's messages to the last remaining churches in Asia – and indeed also how Paul wrote: *"all who are in Asia turned away from me"* (2 Timothy 1:15). This was nothing other than a retreat from the things Paul and the other apostles had faithfully taught – as you can see from the context. And so this meant, without a doubt, that the spiritual house was in decline like its Old Testament physical predecessor. Shortly afterwards, biblically recognisable churches of God went totally out of existence. Historians have written about the ensuing so-called 'Dark Ages' – dark because of the loss of spiritual light from God's Word. But brighter times lay ahead in God's grace. Biblical truth began to be restored from the time of the Reformation until it once again became possible for there to be churches of God out of the same original biblical mould as the very first of these at Jerusalem.

CHAPTER EIGHT: THE HOPE OF THE HEBREWS LETTER

I'd like to introduce this chapter with a verse from Hebrews 3:6: *"Christ ... as Son over His house; whose house are we, if we hold fast our boldness and the glorying of our hope firm unto the end"* (Hebrews 3:6).

Notice the word 'hope' there. I'd like to distinguish between two different hopes in the New Testament. First, there's what we might term 'the Gospel hope.' Various verses give different angles on this. Titus 2:13 describes the promised return of Jesus Christ as being the Christian believer's *'blessed hope'*. Closely connected with that return will be our going to heaven, where Peter tells us there's an inheritance reserved for us as *"a living hope which can never fade away"* (1 Peter 1:3-4).

But the hope in the verse we read from Hebrews is different from that Gospel hope which is to be realized in the future. This hope in Hebrews is a present thing, which is clear from the fact that we're told to hold on to it – that is to hold onto our actual experience of it now. That's what makes it different. We can't week-by-week experience the 'rapture event' (as the return of Christ for his Church is often called), nor can we yet experience our heavenly inheritance, but we can get involved in the actual experience and enjoyment of this Hebrews' hope.

Chapter 6 of Hebrews tells us a bit more about it. The hope is traced back to the sure blessing of Abraham which is described again here so that ... *"we who have taken refuge would have strong encouragement to take hold of the hope set before us. This hope we have as an anchor of the soul, a hope both sure and steadfast and one which enters within the veil, where Jesus has entered as a forerunner for us, having become a high priest forever"* (Hebrews 6:18-20).

In olden times a small boat would go on ahead of a larger ship, carrying its anchor into the harbour. Jesus as our high priest has entered into the sanctuary of heaven before us. Our hope in him as a forerunner is an anchor of our soul. It's sure and steadfast, and is all bound up with our present worship experience of accessing beyond the veil in the heavenly sanctuary as we come to God as his people in worship.

The context here is the Holy Spirit's appeal throughout this Hebrews' letter. There are five major warnings that God's New Testament people – and the Jews among them especially – should not exit from the churches of God so as to go back to the old ways of Judaism of the pre-Christian era. If they did so, he warns, they would miss out on the magnificent spiritual counterpart of so much of the Old Testament system when God's house on earth was a physical temple, such as that built by Solomon. It had an earthly sanctuary, its holy of holies where the Ark of the Covenant was housed, but the spiritual house or temple we began by reading about has its sanctuary in heaven. That's where we – according to this hope – go in a spiritual sense when we worship as God's people before him in our remembrance of the Lord Jesus and his once-for-all sacrifice.

So, Jesus in the heavenly sanctuary, and the present invitation to God's spiritual people to draw near there in worship, is what the hope of Hebrews is all about. This is quite distinct from the hope of the Lord's return to this earth in the future. It's our going spiritually into heaven now in the experience of Christian worship. This worship for Christians, spoken about in the Bible, brings us to our theme of God's house. God's temple is the other name given to the place where God's presence is. When we find this spiritual temple mentioned in 1 Corinthians 3:16-17 and in Ephesians 2:21-22, we learn that it was composed of the aggregate of all the local churches of God in New Testament times. False teaching – that which departed from the Apostles' standard teaching – could destroy God's spiritual temple, even as the disobedience of Israel in the past led to God permitting the Babylonians to come and ransack the previous physical temple at Jerusalem. We've referred to the end of Ephesians chapter two, with its reference to God's spiritual temple in the present Church Age, so we should take time to read it. Paul writes to believers in the Church of God at Ephesus and says they are:

"... of the household of God, being built upon the foundation of the apostles and prophets, Christ Jesus himself being the chief corner stone; in whom each several building, fitly framed together, groweth into a holy temple in the Lord; in whom ye also are builded together for a habitation of God in the Spirit" (Ephesians 2:19-22 Revised Version).

Sometimes there's confusion about this ending of Ephesians 2 which talks about each local church fellowship growing up overall into one holy temple. In this case, the Revised Version has the most literal translation of the original language in verse 21, as it refers to many buildings, not one. It envisages local church fellowships like that at Ephesus, and not the one mystical union of Christ's Body. The confusion is that the topic here at the end of chapter two is considered by some to be another description of the Church the Body of Christ. But surely more careful thought shows that could never be.

The church that is Christ's Body – in other words, all believers on the Lord Jesus throughout the Church Age – is never referred to in the Bible as a temple. And, whereas God's temple, as 1 Corinthians 3:17 shows, can be destroyed, the same is not true of the Church which is Christ's body. The Lord himself told us that when he said emphatically in Matthew 16:18, when speaking of it for the first time, that the gates of Hades cannot prevail against it – surely ruling out any thought of it being capable of being destroyed.

And, what's being described in Ephesians 2 has a 'cornerstone'. Does a body have a cornerstone? No. A body has a head, but not a cornerstone. A building, a temple building in particular, has a cornerstone. Back in the time when the Old Testament exiles had returned to Jerusalem and were rebuilding, there was mention of this physically: a chief cornerstone to complete the restoration work on the Temple.

Actually, the language of this concluding section of Ephesians chapter 2 is totally consistent: it mentions house, something that's built, having a foundation, with a cornerstone, made of parts which are framed or fitted together, and is called a temple, a residence for God in the Spirit.

So, now, let's think a bit more about the insight that the one temple is made of component buildings. Because the people in the God's spiritual house are separated geographically from one another and therefore cannot all meet in one place, the one house consists of several parts – one in each city or town where the people live – each one a church of God. An illustration of this is in Matthew 24:1. Jesus came out from the temple and was going away when His disciples came up to point out the temple buildings to Him.

There the Lord Jesus describes the one Jerusalem temple of his time on earth as consisting of several buildings. So this idea is far from new. Another illustration today is a college or university campus. Usually, the departments or faculties for the different subjects are distributed over a wide area, perhaps more than a single campus site, but they're all integrated together and belong to the same overall university.

So, to conclude, I'd like us to look in sequence at what Peter shares in his letter: *"Therefore, putting aside all malice and all deceit and hypocrisy and envy and all slander, like newborn babies, long for the pure milk of the word, so that by it you may grow in respect to salvation, if you have tasted the kindness of the Lord. And coming to Him as to a living stone which has been rejected by men, but is choice and precious in the sight of God, you also, as living stones, are being built up as a spiritual house for a holy priesthood, to offer up spiritual sacrifices acceptable to God through Jesus Christ"* (1 Peter 2:1-5).

I wonder if we can see four steps there in the construction of God's spiritual house? We can compare those steps with what we read before in 1 Kings 6:7 – when Solomon built its physical predecessor at Jerusalem. Remember, in our previous studies, we've observed how stones for that building project were cut or quarried, then shaped or prepared, then brought on site and added together, so that finally they could be built up as God's temple. By analogy, we may like to compare how individual living stones are made alive by being born again (1 Peter 1:23) by the grace of God (verse 3; also Ephesians 2:8). In that sense they were quarried at Calvary's cross.

Then individual living stones, by reading, growing and experiencing the Lord, are shaped or prepared for service (which is ongoing; v.2). The Lord then adds them individually to the existing structure made out of living, shaped stones which have been aligned to the Chief corner stone, Christ – as head of the corner (verse 4). It's all built on the foundation, which is the teaching of Christ which was laid by the apostles and prophets in early New Testament times (1 Corinthians 3:10,11; Ephesians 2:20). And so, as with the physical temple of the Old Testament, the stones here are again built up and established as the one and only holy temple (Ephesians 2:22).

CHAPTER NINE: FITTING ALL THE FUNCTIONS TOGETHER

A definition: the house of God is the place on earth where God can dwell among his people. There can only be one house of God on earth at any one time.

An individual person can function in many different ways during his or her lifetime. For example, a particular man may be a husband, a father, an employee and a taxpayer. Although these all describe the same person, and are all true simultaneously, they're not the same function.

Similarly, the house of God functions in different specific ways on the earth: for example, as a people, a people for God – set apart for him and distinct from all other people on earth. But it also serves as a kingdom, God's kingdom – one which acknowledges the authority of Christ. And functions by carrying out the responsibilities that come from being a priesthood that is to God and for God – serving him in all the ways he's specified in his Word

These functions are all distinct from each other, and yet they all apply simultaneously to the house of God. Perhaps, it might help to picture this relationship by imagining a cube, like a die. Instead of the numbers one to six on its faces, try to imagine looking at a die with three faces visible: one forward-facing and to the left; another forward-facing and to the right; and one on top. Now if we think of that die or cube as God's house, I would like to ask you to imagine that on those three visible faces are displayed respectively the descriptions: the kingdom of God, the priesthood, and the people of God.

We should further clarify our terms here. By the term people of God, is meant those possessed by God, and separated to God. By the term kingdom of God, is meant those who acknowledge the rule and authority exercised by God. And, finally, by the term priesthood, is meant those who offer service for God.

In relation to each of the three functions of the house, and the house itself, Jesus is prominent and is known by a particularly relevant title in each case. According to Hebrews 3:6, he is *'son over God's house.'* According to Hebrews 2:11 and 13:12, he is the leader of the congregation of God's gathered people. According to Hebrews 3:1 and 10:21, he's the great high priest over the priestly house. And, according to Matthew 28:18, Jesus is king, the one having all authority in God's kingdom.

We're using New Testament verses, of course, as we're anxious to understand the direct relevance of all this for today. But it's good, as we conclude our Bible-wide review of this major theme with its dramatic implications for our Christian discipleship, that we see the symmetry with the Old Testament. The teaching of both parts of the Bible blend into an overall bigger picture which is a vital reassurance. Reassurance - why do I say that?

Well, how does one gain reassurance about the teaching of any verse? It's by comparing other Bible passages on the same topic. Laying one thing alongside another was one method of the earliest Bible teachers when they were expounding scripture (Acts 17:3). In reality, it's the same thing you face when wondering if it would be correct to fit the next piece of the jigsaw puzzle in one particular place. How do you get assurance in that situation – about whether you're attempting to fit the correct piece in the correct place? You simply stand back and take in an overview of the whole picture.

Each piece of the puzzle carries a tiny part of the overall picture. Only when they're all in the correct places, will that perfect complete picture emerge which compares with the puzzle solution guide. Now we come back to apply our analogy to the study of our Bible. When we ask ourselves: 'Have I understood that verse correctly, as God wants me to?' What we have to do is step back and see the bigger Bible picture – and ask: how does my interpretation of what this one verse says fit with God's mainline purposes as the Bible overall reveals them?

We need to do that now, as we approach the conclusion of this study. If the present day application of this matters for our service – and it does – how can we be sure we've got it right? This is the reason why this series has taken a Bible-wide panorama. Now, take our current topic: about the three functions closely related to being God's house. Is it possible to find a correspondence between God's purposes – between his intentional dealings with men and women - in the Old Testament as compared with his purposes in New Testament times?

Well, I want to take you to inspect side by side one Old Testament text and one New Testament text. The one from the Old Testament is from Exodus 19:

"Now then, if you will indeed obey My voice and keep My covenant, then you shall be My own possession among all the peoples, for all the earth is Mine; and you shall be to Me a kingdom of priests and a holy nation.' These are the words that you shall speak to the sons of Israel. Let them construct a sanctuary for Me, that I may dwell among them. According to all that I am going to show you, as the pattern of the tabernacle and the pattern of all its furniture, just so you shall construct it." (Exodus 19:5-9)

Looking back over those words we've read from Exodus 19, we hear the same things we've been talking about, but coming also from Old Testament times. The nation of Israel was chosen by God to be: the people of God; a kingdom; and a priesthood – even as they were those identified with the construction of God's sanctuary or house. It was to be constructed, so they could function in those previously mentioned ways as the people of God; a kingdom; and a priesthood.

Now we'll travel over to New Testament times, and to First Peter chapter 2, where we read: *"you also, as living stones, are being built up as a spiritual house for a holy priesthood, to offer up spiritual sacrifices acceptable to God through Jesus Christ. But you are A CHOSEN RACE, A royal PRIESTHOOD, A HOLY NATION, A PEOPLE FOR God's OWN POSSESSION, so that you may proclaim the excellencies of Him who has called you out of darkness into His marvelous light; for you once were NOT A PEOPLE, but now you are THE PEOPLE OF GOD; you had not received mercy, but now you have received mercy"* (1 Peter 2:5,9-10).

There are plainly terms there that we should recognize. Associated with being God's house – now a spiritual house – there are nevertheless the same duties or functions. There's mention of a holy nation or people who are God's prized possession, and mention of a priesthood that is both holy and royal.

But let's read other New Testament verses which pair together different combinations of these functions of God's house which we're considering. We'll do this to emphasize the inter-relatedness of all these things, so as to show that it's one and the same company of persons which is always in view in the New Testament. We begin with: *"...for we are the temple of the living God; just as God said, "I will dwell in them and walk among them; and I will be their God, and they shall be My PEOPLE"* (2 Corinthians 6:16) and observe that this links God's house or temple to those who are God's people. Okay, now we'll take our next reading in Acts 14:

"...strengthening the souls of the disciples, encouraging them to continue in the faith, and saying, 'Through many tribulations we must enter the kingdom of God.' [It says] When they had appointed elders for them in every church, having prayed with fasting, they commended them to the Lord in whom they had believed." (Acts 14:22-23)

And we notice there the side by side mentions of God's kingdom on the one hand, and on the other hand, disciples continuing in the faith taught by elders in every church, all of which together formed God's house. We now come to *"... you also, as living stones, are being built up as a spiritual house for a holy priesthood, to offer up spiritual sacrifices acceptable to God through Jesus Christ"* (1 Peter 2:5).

Clearly, this links God's spiritual house to the priesthood function. Now we come to the Lord's words: *"Do not be afraid, LITTLE FLOCK, for your Father has chosen gladly to give you the KINGDOM."* (Luke 12:32) Which links a people being led like a flock to its overall kingdom function. Let's look now at: *"But you are A CHOSEN RACE, A royal PRIESTHOOD, A HOLY NATION, A PEOPLE FOR God's OWN POSSESSION, so that you may proclaim the excellencies of Him who has called you out of darkness into His marvelous light ..."* (1 Peter 2:9).

This reference binds together the function of God's people and the priesthood. And finally, *"and He has made us to be a kingdom, priests to His God and Father - to Him be the glory and the dominion forever and ever. Amen"* (Revelation 1:6). This links the kingdom aspect to the priesthood aspect.

Since all these vital aspects of corporate Christian service are bound together in these ways and centred on God's house, it emphasizes once again how important a topic of study this is. The entire vision of God as expressed throughout the New Testament is satisfied in the reality of what we find: born-again believers, baptized by immersion in water as disciples of the Lord Jesus, in faithful adherence to the teaching of the Apostles, and maintained in this unifying focus by the supervision of caring elders in every location in which the overall community expressed itself - and all the while standing in dedicated separation to God from worldly associations.

To quote Jacob again from Genesis 28:17: *"How awesome is this place! This is none other than the house of God, and this is the gate of heaven."*

QUESTIONS FOR STUDY AND REFLECTION

1) Some Bible verses with the word 'church' follow. Into which of these six categories (grouping of trades-people; encampment of Israel; the body of all believers; the local biblical church fellowship of disciples; the overall people / household of God; and a heavenly gathering of angels) does each fall? Acts 11:22; 1 Corinthians 11:22; Ephesians 1:22

2) The Church the body of Christ is referred to (usually directly) in the following 21 verses: Matthew 16:17; Matthew 16:18; John 1:33; Acts 2:1,4; Romans 12:5 12:4; I Corinthians 12:4; 1 Corinthians 12:7; I Corinthians 12:13; 2 Corinthians 5:17; Galatians 3:28; Ephesians 3:3; Ephesians 3:9,21; Ephesians 3:11; Ephesians 4:4; Ephesians 5:23; Ephesians 5:25; Ephesians 5:27; Ephesians 5:30; Ephesians 5:32; 1 Thessalonians 4:16; Genesis 24:15,16

There now follow 24 descriptions of the Church which is the body of Christ. For each statement below, find a supporting Scripture from the list above (some Scriptures support more than one description):

1. There is only one 'church which is Christ's body'.

2. It began at Pentecost with the coming of the Holy Spirit.

3. It will be complete at 'the rapture' when the church will be taken from the world.

4. Born-again believers are members of the body.

5. They are made members by being baptized (spiritually) in the Holy Spirit into the body.

6. Christ does the baptizing ...

7. ...because He himself is building this church.

8. It includes all who are 'in Christ', whether dead or alive.

9. At the rapture, the dead in Christ will be raised so that when Christ meets His church for the first time, it will be complete.

10. It is perfect and glorious, and cannot be marred by sin or Satan.

11. Christ will present it to Himself as a bride, absolutely spotless.

12. It is a mystery hidden from many people today and from everyone in Old Testament times.

13. God planned it in eternity past.

14. He gave illustrations of it in the Old Testament (e.g. Rebekah).

15. Christ mentioned it first when speaking to Peter.

16. It was fully disclosed to the apostle Paul (who then taught it to others).

17. It is revealed to certain people now by God.

18. It will last eternally.

19. Christ is head of this church.

20. The members of it are members of each other

21. There is no distinction in membership or human authority within it.

22. Christ loves the church, and died for it.

23. Every member of it has received a spiritual gift.

24. The members do not all have the same gift.

3. There follows a list of characteristics of the churches of God which are different from the above characteristics of the Church the Body of Christ. Match the Scriptures shown below with the characteristics to which they refer.

1. They are on earth and visible.

2. They are imperfect.

3. There are more than one.

4. They are linked in a fellowship.

5. There is no more than one in a city.

6. Each one has a beginning ...

7. ... and may have an end.

8. Individuals must be added to it

9. Not all believers are in the churches of God

10. They are strengthened by the exercise of spiritual gifts.

11. They can be persecuted ...

12. ... and made havoc of.

13. Discipline and judgement must be carried out within them

14. There are distinctions made between men and women.

15. There are distinctions in responsibility.

16. They consist of those who are 'in the Lord'.

Acts 2:41; Acts 8:1; Acts 11:26; 1 Corinthians 1:9; 1 Corinthians 3:10; 1 Corinthians 5:3; 1 Corinthians 15:9; 2 Corinthians 11:28; Galatians 1:13; Philippians 1:1; 1 Thessalonians 1:1; 1 Thessalonians 5:12; 1 Timothy 2:8,9; Revelation 2:5; Revelation 3:2

4. Give some reasons why being in the Church the Body of Christ is not the same as being in a church of God.

5. What reasons, in your opinion, do Christians use in deciding which church group to belong to? Which of them are valid?

6. What answers would you give to a Christian friend who said: "I prefer to serve God by myself; I'm freer that way"?

7. What principles of God's residence among humans on earth are advanced in the account of Jacob's dream at Bethel?

8. In 2 Samuel 6:1-10, we read of king David's desire to bring the Ark of the covenant from the house of Abinadab to its proper place in the Tabernacle. However he neglected to comply with God's law in Numbers 4:15 as to HOW it should be done, with the result that Uzzah lost his life. What lessons can we learn from this with respect to our desire to do the Lord's will today?

9. How is the change in God's House from Old Testament to New Testament shown in each of the following Scriptures? Matthew 23:38; Mark 12:1-11; Luke 12:32; Acts 4:11; 1 Peter 2:6,7

10. Describe how each of these four steps has its parallel or counterpart in the construction of the Temple which Solomon built (see 1 Kings 6:7): Made into living stones (v.1); made ready as building material (v.2); added to the Lord (v.4); and so built up as God's spiritual house (v.5).

11. By studying carefully the ending of Ephesians chapter 2, make sure you can support the translation / interpretation of 'oikos' as 'house' (as distinct from the other possibility of 'family'). Try to do this by appealing - in context - to the nearby mention of a 'foundation' & 'corner-stone'.

12. In what respects is God's house in the Old Testament (firstly the tabernacle, then Solomon's temple) similar to and different from God's house in the New Testament (the community of churches of God)?

13. What particular aspects or functions of the house of God are emphasized in these verses? Ephesians 2:21-22; 1 Timothy 3:15; Hebrews 10:21-22; 1 Peter 2:5; 1 Peter 4:17

14. Is God's house today something that is important to you – why or why not?

MORE TITLES IN THIS SERIES

If you've enjoyed reading this book, first of all please consider taking a moment to leave a positive review where you purchased this book! Secondly, you may be interested to know that, at the date of the publishing of this book, the Search For Truth library now stands at over fifty ebook titles; each contains excellent reading material in a down-to-earth and conversational style, covering a wide range of topics from Bible character studies, theme studies, book studies, apologetics, prophecy, Christian living and more. The books can be found online simply by searching for the specific title or "Brian Johnston Search For Truth Series" online. Paperback versions of some titles can also be purchased from Hayes Press at www.hayespress.org. A flavour of some of the books in the library is below:

Healthy Churches: God's Bible Blueprint For Growth (FREE EBOOK)

As Brian notes in the opening chapters of this book, many churches in the Western world seem to be declining in numbers and spiritual vitality. He explores some of the root causes and also how this trend could be reversed. The good news, as Brian reminds us, is that God gives us the growth blueprint in His Word through a number of key Bible words, such as sowing, reaping, planting, watering, cultivating, building and edifying. Find out the importance of each step in the process and get inspired to go for growth with, in and through, God!

Hope For Humanity: God's Fix for a Broken World

Daily headlines remind us that this world is broken in so many different ways; an honest look within ourselves reveals deep problems there as well. This book pinpoints the same cause behind both and rejects all man-made solutions in favour of the divine one – the sending of His Son at Bethlehem on a mission that would lead to a cross at Calvary – with a challenge to every reader to accept or reject it. A very conversational book, full of anecdotes and illustrations, yet direct and challenging - ideal to share with someone you know who you wish to reach with the good news of Jesus Christ, or to strengthen and sharpen your own faith in the gospel.

Tomorrow's Headlines – Bible Prophecy

This e-book provides some key principles for unlocking the meaning of Bible prophecy and surveys what the Bible says about the future, primarily from the books of Daniel and Revelation.

Overcoming Objections to Christian Faith

This e-book provides a concise introduction to answering 10 key objections to the Christian faith by giving number of insightful illustrations and Biblical references which all Christians can use to help them give "a reason for the hope that is within us" and whet the appetite for further research on each question in greater depth.

Abraham – Friend of God

Brian Johnston's provides an informative biography and commentary of one of the most important characters in the Old Testament of our Bibles – Abraham the nomad. Abraham was known for his great example of faith and for being a "Friend of God", but his life was far from plain sailing. Brian draws out a number of lessons for our discipleship today in this helpful Bible study.

James – The Epistle of Straw?

Martin Luther didn't seem overly impressed with the Bible letter by James, describing it as 'a right strawy epistle'! It seems he felt disappointed that it didn't contain any exalted description of Christ, nor make reference to the work of the Spirit, and didn't work hard to defend the faith. It's true that James doesn't deal with the glories of Christ and his Church or with the great Christian blessings, nor does he transport us to the world to come. James seems to be at home in more mundane matters. He doesn't write in great soaring passages, nor are there many strongly motivating exhortations. But the value of his contribution, under God, is in forcing us to face up squarely to practical realities and their ethical implications. Brian brings us face to face with these realities in a down to earth style that perhaps James himself would have appreciated!

Once Saved, Always Saved...

The issue of whether a Christian can lose their salvation is an absolutely critical one and has been a controversial topic amongst

Christians for centuries. This book provides a number of insightful illustrations and Biblical references which all Christians can use to reassure themselves that there is no basis in the Bible for the so-called "Falling Away Doctrine" and that, once saved, a believer can never be lost under any circumstances.

Double Vision – The Insights of Isaiah

The Old Testament book of Isaiah can be difficult to understand. This book provides the key to open up Isaiah's message by explaining the "double vision" model that God used in speaking through the prophet. While what much of what Isaiah said had a current application to the people he was speaking to, there was usually a double meaning which either spoke of the coming of Jesus Christ hundreds of years later, or of events which are still yet in our future. This short book is bound to leave you more aware of, and appreciating more fully, the sovereignty of God and his gracious dealings with both Israel and followers of Jesus Christ.

Other Titles

- An Unchanging God?
- The Kingdom of God – Past, Present or Future?
- God's Appointment Calendar: The Feasts of Jehovah
- Seeds – A Potted Bible History
- AWOL! Bible Deserters and Defectors
- The Way – New Testament Discipleship
- 5 Sacred Solos – The Truths That The Reformation Recovered
- Salt & The Sacrifice of Christ

- Turning The World Upside Down – Seven Revolutionary Ideas That Changed The World
- Windows To Faith
- The Visions of Zechariah
- Stronger Than the Storm - The Last Words of Jesus
- Closer Than A Brother – Christian Friendship
- Experiencing God in Ephesians
- About The Bush – The Life of Moses
- Trees of the Bible
- After God's Own Heart: The Life of David
- Knowing God: Reflections on Psalm 23
- They Met at the Cross: Five Encounters With Jesus
- Pure Milk: Nurturing New Life in Jesus
- A Legacy of Kings – Israel's Chequered History
- Edge of Eternity – Approaching the End of Life
- Fencepost Turtles – People Placed by God
- Living in God's House: His Design in Action
- Jesus: What Does The Bible Really Say?
- No Compromise!
- First Corinthians – Nothing But Christ Crucified
- The Glory of God
- Jesus: Son Over God's House
- The Tabernacle: God's House of Shadows
- Esther: A Date With Destiny
- Power Outage: Christianity Unplugged
- Life, the Universe and Ultimate Answers
- The Supremacy of Christ
- Samson: A Type of Christ
- Pure Christianity: The Essence of Biblical Discipleship
- Praying with Paul
- Unlocking Hebrews
- Minor Prophets, Major Issues!
- Five Women and a Baby – The Genealogy of Jesus
- Bible Answers for Big Questions

SEARCH FOR TRUTH RADIO BROADCASTS

Search for Truth Radio has been a ministry of the Churches of God since 1978. Free Search for Truth podcasts can be listened to online or downloaded at www.searchfortruth.podbean.com, or via the ITunes podcast app, or at our website – www.churchesofgod.info. If you have enjoyed reading one of our books or listening to a radio broadcast, we would love to know about that, or answer any questions that you might have.

Contact us at:

The Barn, Flaxlands, Royal Wootton Basset, Wiltshire Swindon, SN4 8DY, UK

P.O. Box 748, Ringwood, Victoria 3134, Australia

P.O. Box 70115, Chilomoni, Blantyre, Malawi

Web site: www.searchfortruth.org.uk

Email: sft@churchesofgod.info

Also, if you have enjoyed reading this book and or others in the series, we would really appreciate it if you could just take a couple of minutes to leave a brief review where you purchased this book – it really is a very good way of spreading the word about our ministry – thanks and God bless!

Did you love *Living in God's House: His Design in Action*? Then you should read *First Corinthians: Nothing But Christ Crucified* by Brian Johnston!

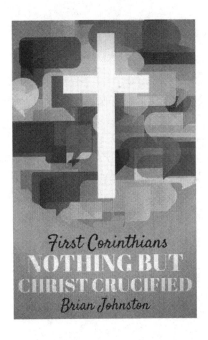

Bible teacher Brian Johnston unpacks the first letter of the apostle Paul to the Corinthians in this informative book, exploring such important topics as spiritual gifts, the body of Christ, headcoverings, the Breaking of Bread and the powerful wisdom of God in Christ crucified!

Read more at amzn.to/1u7rzIA.

About the Author

Born and educated in Scotland, Brian worked as a government scientist until God called him into full-time Christian ministry on behalf of the Churches of God (www.churchesofgod.info). His voice has been heard on Search For Truth radio broadcasts for over 30 years during which time he has been an itinerant Bible teacher throughout the UK and Canada. His evangelical and missionary work outside the UK is primarily in Belgium and The Philippines. He is married to Rosemary, with a son and daughter.

Read more at amzn.to/1u7rzIA.

About the Publisher

Hayes Press (www.hayespress.org) is a registered charity in the United Kingdom, whose primary mission is to disseminate the Word of God, mainly through literature. It is one of the largest distributors of gospel tracts and leaflets in the United Kingdom, with over 100 titles and hundreds of thousands despatched annually.

Hayes Press also publishes Plus Eagles Wings, a fun and educational Bible magazine for children, six times a year and Golden Bells, a popular daily Bible reading calendar in wall or desk formats.

Also available are over 100 Bibles in many different versions, shapes and sizes, Christmas cards, Christian jewellery, Eikos Bible Art, Bible text posters and much more!